Jumping
The Moon

Jumping The Moon

Written by Bobbie Cromer
& Illustrated by Madison Feldhaus

Jumping the Moon
Copyright © 2018 by Bobbie Cromer

All rights reserved. This book or any portion thereof may not be reproduced or used in any manner whatsoever without the express written permission of the publisher except for the use of brief quotations in a book review.

Published June 2018

Illustrated by Madison Feldhaus
madisonfeldhaus.com

ISBN: 978-1719441841

It is hard to believe that a pony like me could one day become a show pony. After all, I am a mustang -- a wild mustang! Born into the White Mountain Herd on the plains of Wyoming, I was meant to live wild and free, as my ancestors lived for thousands of years. That is how I spent the first three years of my life, until one hot summer morning when my life changed.

The other horses and I were just waking up while the stallion of our herd watched over us. Danger is always present in the wild so we were always alert for predators. In the distance we heard a strange whirring noise. The skies were filled with whirling helicopters which were headed straight toward us, low to the ground and rocking back and forth. The herd and I galloped away.

Mile after mile we ran, our hooves pounding the earth, our eyes wide with terror. I thought we were never going to stop running when suddenly we had nowhere to go. We were hundreds of horses driven into a pen; tired, dazed and frightened. I knew the herd and I had lost our freedom once the gates closed behind us. Everything had changed. We had nowhere to run, no mountain streams from which to drink. There would be no more grazing the wild plains.

We were never again to roam free like our ancestors had for so many years.

The following day we were branded. I was branded on the left side of my neck. The brand showed that we were the property of the United States Government. The symbols told our age, the state where we were brought after our capture, and a four letter code which identified us until our adoption, if we were lucky enough to find a home. Our brands also mean we are no longer wild mustangs, we are just mustangs!

I waited every day, hoping someone would adopt me. Thankfully, that person came. His name was Joe Williams. Joe was a horse trainer from Ocala, Florida who had trained other mustangs before me. I was a lucky boy; luckier than I would ever know for my adoption was an opportunity for a new life. I was scared, but my instinct told me, this man would be good to me. That proved to be true, for the time I spent with Joe made me the pony I am today.

Joe loaded me and other mustangs into a large horse trailer and we were off to Ocala, Florida. The ride wasn't too bad. I had lots of hay to eat and the other horses around me kept me calm. I had a lot to think about on the ride. I realized that I now had to depend on someone else for the things I used to do for myself, such as providing me with food, water and shelter.

The long trip ended late at night. Joe and I were both tired as he gently pulled me out of the trailer and put me in a stall. That was the first time in my life I had ever been in a horse stall. I could hear other horses in the surrounding stalls, as I lay down in the soft straw. The nearness of the other mustangs brought me comfort and I knew I was in a safe place.

Morning came quickly and before I knew it the sun was poking through my window. Joe came to my stall door and said, " So Holy Smokes, how was your first night?"

Holy Smokes? Was that me? I heard him call to the other horses by name, so I guessed I was Holy Smokes! Joe talked to me as he put something in my bucket called sweet feed. Oh boy! It was the best food I ever tasted.

Later that day, Joe came and led me out to a round fenced-in enclosure called a round pen. I trotted round and round. Joe kept throwing a rope out toward me to keep me moving. I was used to being with a herd and having a leader. I wasn't used to being by myself. I felt scared and alone. I licked my lips and lowered my head. Joe stopped throwing the rope at me, walked to the center of the ring, turned his back to me and just stood there. I wasn't sure what to do, but I wanted to be near him. I wanted a leader. Slowly, I walked to him and put my head on his shoulder. Joe turned and stroked my neck. I felt happy. Everything was going to be OK. What occurred between Joe and me is called "Joining Up". I had accepted him as my leader.

Everyday after that, we worked in the round pen or in the training ring. I would jump over poles or go between barrels. Sometimes Joe would wrap a rope around my legs and then throw it over my head or my back. All this was done so I would learn to stay calm and not jump at every new obstacle I encountered.

One day Joe very slowly laid over my back. I had never had anything on my back before. It is against a horse's nature to have anything on our back for that is where our enemies such as a cougar, or a mountain lion, would attack us. I tried hard to stay calm, but fear took over and I bucked Joe right off into the dirt. He got up laughing and said we could try again tomorrow.

There were lots of tomorrows. I was taught to accept a bit in my mouth, to allow a bridle over my head, to pick up my feet so he could clean them, and to stand still while I was being groomed. The hardest lesson of all was to allow a person to sit on my back. This took a while, but I finally learned to trust.

Joe was the best trainer this pony could have every hoped for. He taught me to walk, trot, canter, lay down on the ground, and stand on a little box. He made me a talented little mustang.

Give ponies a clean place to live, feed us, be patient and kind and we will repay your kindness. Joe did these things for me and I have him to thank for making me into the pony I am today. I am a lucky boy!

We were even in a rodeo! Joe rode me bareback with just a rope around my neck to guide me. I stood on the little box. I jumped over low jumps and the crowd cheered. I loved showing off what I had learned from Joe. He was so proud and I was so happy.

There were two people watching me that day at the rodeo, they owned a riding stable in Pennsylvania. That day when they saw me in the rodeo, "I just have to have that pony. He is amazing!"

That day when they saw me in the rodeo, they thought I was amazing and told Joe they wanted to take me back to their farm.

The morning after the rodeo Joe told me that the time had come for me to do what he had trained me to be, a show pony. That afternoon they came to bring me to their farm. As they led me into their trailer I turned back to look at Joe. This was the man who changed my life. I would miss him.

We finally arrived after a long ride. As we approached the winding driveway I looked out my trailer window and saw beautiful green pastures with streams running through them. I knew this was going to be a great place to live. All the children at the farm were excited to see me, they were jumping up and down trying to peek into the trailer.

After I was unloaded from the trailer I was taken to a beautiful green pasture, so that I could get used to my new home. Horses were everywhere: in the paddocks running free, in the stalls eating hay, in the riding rings taking lessons with little girls and boys. I, Holy Smokes, was a part of this.

I was a lucky boy. I spent most of my days in the paddock or in my new stall. I was happy but felt something was missing. Nobody was riding me. I heard someone say, I was too "green". That meant I was too inexperienced to be a lesson pony, so I spent a lot of time alone.

I watched a spunky, little ten year old girl, named Remy whenever she came to the barn. Remy took lessons on all the different lesson ponies. They were named Skittles, Coco, Apple Pie and Macaroni. Remy was always giggling and spinning around. She always had the biggest smile on her face when riding any one of these ponies. She was sweet to the ponies. Always brushing them and talking to them about going to the horse shows. Remy loved to jump the ponies; the higher the better. She realized that none of the lesson ponies could jump as high as she wanted to go.

One afternoon I heard her trainer, Dana, say, "Remy why don't you try Holy Smokes? He can jump the moon." My ears pricked up. Maybe, I was going to get my turn in the training ring. My chance had finally come. I could now show them what Joe had taught me. The next day Remy came to my stall and gave my face a little rub. "Hello Smokey, I am Remy. Why don't you and I give it a try together."

I could tell she was nervous. So was I. First, I had to be groomed, so she brushed and brushed until I gleamed. The entire time Remy talked to me. Her words calmed me. Later, I learned that Remy could talk a lot. Next, she saddled me up and I was ready to take my first lesson.

Dana, the trainer, told us to walk. "Okay, I can do this," I thought to myself. Trotting came next. I could feel Remy posting up and down as I moved. She was light as a feather. I loved this! I was feeling so good.

I gave a few little bucks. Remy just laughed and kept riding and talking to me. Then, it was canter. This was more like it! I loved going fast, but Remy kept saying, "Whoa," to slow me down. She said, "Whoa," a lot. The next part of our lesson was jumping. Dana set up a few low jumps. Remy and I sailed over them easily. The next jumps Dana set up were higher and we cleared them all. Remy and I were a team.

Remy asked Dana if she could ride in the next show. Dana said that we would have to practice together more if we were to go to a show.

Over the next couple of weeks we sure did practice. Every day we would go in the ring to walk, trot, canter and jump. Occasionally I would get a little ornery and take off galloping. Remy would just laugh and go along for the ride. I was happy being with her and she took good care of me. I never looked better, if I do say so myself.

The day of the show finally arrived. I was bathed, brushed and fussed over so much by Remy and her Mom that you could tell how much my appearance meant to them. Remy said, she wanted me to be a Rock Star. Whatever that meant? That morning I was loaded onto the trailer with some of the other ponies and off we went. When I arrived, I saw Remy waiting for me. She took me off the trailer and brought me to a place on the grass and proceeded to saddle me.

Wow! We were off the to warm-up ring. I was so nervous. I began trotting in all directions. "Calm down, Smokey, everything will be Ok," said Remy. Just hearing her voice calmed me down. Next thing I knew, we were entering the Show Ring as the announcer said, "Let's all congratulate Remy on her purchase of Holy Smokes." I was Remy's pony? Holy Smokes! Crying tears of happiness Remy laid her head on my neck. I got a little teary eyed myself but knew we had to start the course.

I gave a few little bounces to get her to sit up. She gathered the reins and we were off toward the first jump. "You can do it Smokey," Remy yelled. Then she yelled "Jump" then "Jump" again. Before I knew it, we had finished the course. "Good boy, Smokey," Remy shouted as she patted my neck. It was at that moment I got a peculiar feeling but didn't know what it was. I only knew that it felt good.

We had won First Place! It was to be the first of many First Place finishes. Remy kissed me all over my face. I was a little embarrassed. When it was time to put the Blue Ribbon on the side of my face, I had to draw the line. Mustangs don't wear ribbons! I jumped up and down until finally Remy put the ribbon on the top of her boot and laughed. It was a good day.

That summer passed with more practice, more lessons, and more fun. Every day, I was with my best friend. We took care of each other. I did my part by getting her over the jumps and she did hers by guiding me safely through the course. I guess one could say that we were "Besties".

Each morning, Remy would come to the pasture and yell, "Smokey! Come on boy!" I would look up and walk to her. If the other horses in the field were following, I would stop and wait until they turned around, as it was too dangerous for all of us to be at the gate because Remy could get hurt. I have to watch out for her too!

Only once in a while when I was feeling lazy, did I run away from her. Remy knew how to fix that. She just got that bucket of grain and I was right there. I tried to tell her that I was sorry by nudging her with my head, but she would ignore me, although I knew that by the time we got to the schooling ring she would be patting my neck and telling me what a good boy I was – even though I could be a bit "spicy" at times.

It has been a year now and Remy and I have become quite a team. For example, at one of the fancier shows, we were competing against all breeds of horses, and people of every age. Remy was the youngest, being only ten. As we were approaching the gate to enter the Show Ring, I saw the looks on the other riders' faces, as if they were thinking, "What is that mustang pony doing with that little girl in this class?" We answered that question by winning First Place and **Grand Champion**!

That just proves, you may not be the fanciest or best looking pony, and even a mustang, or you may just be a little girl, but when you have heart and determination, you can achieve whatever you set out to do.

Remy and I have learned, we are not always perfect but we try. We may not always come in First Place but what matters most is that we have each other. There is a wonderful feeling between us that I had felt before but didn't know what it was. It is love!

This little, wild mustang has been transformed into a much loved Show Pony. My destiny was to find Remy, who needed me as much as I needed her. Every horse or pony needs a person, and I've got Remy. I would do anything for her. If she asked me to jump the Moon, I would try.

Who knows? Maybe one night you will look up and see the silhouette of a horse and rider jumping over the Moon and you will know just who it is!

About the Author: Bobbie Cromer

Bobbie lives in Upstate New York and is a horse lover and true advocate for their welfare. She is a long time volunteer at Old Friends at Cabin Creek, a racehorse retirement farm. Bobbie is a strong believer that horses need to be cared for their whole lives.

Jumping the Moon is a story inspired by her granddaughter's mustang, Holy Smokes, and his journey from a wild mustang to a successful show pony. The story is about love, trust and the belief that no matter who or what you are, you can achieve your dreams.

A portion of the proceeds of the sale of this book will be donated to The mustang Heritage Foundation and Old Friends at Cabin Creek

Remy and Smokey

Photo by Andrew Ryback

Made in the USA
San Bernardino, CA
25 June 2018